William and Kate

BY DALE-MARIE BRYAN

The Child's World

Published by The Child's World®
1980 Lookout Drive • Mankato, MN 56003-1705
800-599-READ • www.childsworld.com

Acknowledgments
The Child's World®: Mary Berendes, Publishing Director
The Design Lab: Cover and interior design
Amnet: Cover and interior production
Red Line Editorial: Editorial direction

Photo credits
John Stillwell/AP Images, cover, 1; David Caulkin/AP Images, 5;
Joseph Schaber/AP Images, 7; George Pimentel/WireImage/
Getty Images, 9; The Canadian Press, Frank Gunn/AP Images, 11;
Lynne Sladky/AP Images, 13; Ian Jones/AP Images, 15; Joel Robine/
AP Images, 17; Frank Gunn/The Canadian Press/AP Images, 19;
Toby Melville/WPA Solo Rota/AP Images, 21; Stephen Finn/
Shutterstock Images, 23; GYI NSE/iStockphoto, 25; Featureflash/
Shutterstock Images, 27, 29

Design elements
Sergey Shvedov/iStockphoto

ISBN 9781614732877
LCCN 2012933739

Printed in the United States of America
Mankato, MN
July 2012
PA02128

Table of Contents

CHAPTER 1

Once Upon a Time

Once upon a time—January 9, 1982, to be exact—a fairy tale began. That was the day Catherine Elizabeth Middleton was born. A little more than six months later, her prince was born. His parents named him William Arthur Philip Louis. But someday people might call William the King of the United Kingdom of Great Britain and Northern Ireland.

William's mother was Diana, Princess of Wales. People referred to her as

William weighed 7 pounds 1.5 ounces (3.2 kg) when he was born.

Prince William as a baby

Princess Di. She had William on June 21, 1982. William's father is Charles, the Prince of Wales, **heir** to the throne of England. Princess Diana and Prince Charles had another son, Harry, two years later.

CHAPTER 2

Wild Wills

Although he was a prince, William didn't have an easy childhood. His parents were often gone, busy with their royal duties. And his parents didn't get along well. So Harry and Wills, as family and friends called him, were often cared for by nannies.

William's mother said he was "a holy terror." He broke things and slid down the stairs. He also tried to flush his father's shoes and his mother's toothbrush down the toilet.

When William was old enough to go to school, he ordered people around and fought with the other children.

Kate and William are distantly related. They are fifteenth cousins.

Prince William as a child, with a nanny

William attended Mrs. Mynor's Nursery School and then Wetherby School, both in London. Finally, at six, William calmed down. One of his nannies thought it was because he had decided he liked being kind and having good manners. But William was still naughty sometimes. He attacked his father, mother, and even his grandmother the Queen with a squirt gun. And he dropped water balloons from the palace windows.

CHAPTER 3

Party Princess

To the public and press, Catherine is known as
Kate. But her family and friends call her Catherine.
Unlike William, Kate was shy and from an everyday

Kate and her mother, Carole Middleton

family. Her mother was an airline hostess when she met Kate's father. He worked for the airline British Airways. When Kate was two, the family moved to Amman, Jordan. Jordan is a country in the Middle East. Kate went to preschool there at age three.

When they returned to England, Kate's mother and father started a party supply business. It was called Party Pieces. Kate and her sister, Pippa, modeled **tiaras**, princess dresses, and plastic jewelry in pictures for the store. In a few years, the family business was earning millions of dollars. Kate, Pippa, and their little brother James were able to go to the best private schools, which are often expensive.

Kate is 5 feet 10 inches (1.75 m) tall. William is 6 feet 3 inches (1.88 m). He will be the tallest King of England so far.

Kate Grows Up

When Kate was seven, she went to Saint Andrew's School for primary students in Berkshire, England. She excelled in her studies and in sports. Kate did

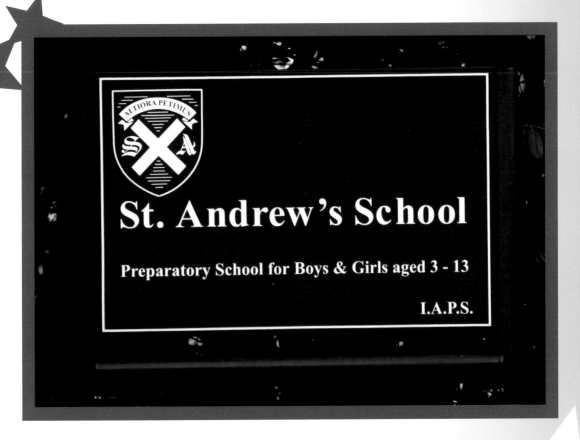

Saint Andrew's School is near the village Pangbourne in the county of Berkshire, England.

well at swimming and track and field. She set a record for the high jump. Though she was quiet, Kate enjoyed being in plays. She was even in a play in which a fortune-teller predicted she would marry a handsome, rich man.

After Saint Andrew's primary school, Kate went to Downe House, an all-girls **boarding school**. Kate was unhappy at Downe. She was homesick and other girls bullied her. Finally, her parents moved her to Marlborough College. But the bullying had made Kate shy.

By 1998, Kate had grown into a beautiful young woman. She was popular. Remembering her own loneliness when she switched schools, she made a point of being friendly to new students.

CHAPTER 5

William's Woes

William attended a boarding school called Ludgrove outside London, and then Eton College in Berkshire. He did well in school, sang solos in music programs,

William *(front)* **with classmates at Eton College boarding school**

and acted in plays. William was the captain of the rugby and soccer teams at Ludgrove. Rugby is similar to football. William also swam and played basketball.

But William had woes, too. The biggest problem was his parents. In 1996, they decided to divorce. From then on, when they were not in school, William and Harry divided their time between Kensington Palace, their mother's home, and Highgrove, where their father lived.

Princess Diana had always been very involved in **charities**. People loved her kind ways and giving nature. She often took the boys with her to homeless shelters, hospitals, and other places people were suffering. Princess Diana wanted her sons to learn what real life was like.

When William was nine, he seriously hurt his skull when he was hit with a golf club.

William plays soccer at Eton College.

CHAPTER 6

William's Tragedy

Being royal made it difficult for William and his family to be in public. The **paparazzi** followed Princess Diana everywhere for pictures. Even though the press had agreed not to bother princes William and Harry, William still worried about his mother. Then, when he was 15, a terrible thing happened.

On August 31, 1997, Princess Diana was killed in a car crash. She was being chased by the paparazzi. Even though police said drunk driving caused the crash, William still blamed the press.

An estimated 2.5 billion people watched Princess Diana's funeral on television.

William *(right)* at his mother's funeral

People worldwide watched the funeral on television. They shared William and Harry's grief. They couldn't believe Princess Diana was gone.

CHAPTER 7

Watching and Waiting

Kate watched Princess Diana's funeral, too. "Those poor boys," she told her mother. For years, Kate had a crush on William, even though she didn't know him. Many people have said that Kate had pictures of the famous prince on her wall in her **dorm** room. But Kate has said that was not true. She did read everything she could about him, though. Kate even told her friends she would marry William someday. Her friends teased her and called her Princess in Waiting.

Kate had a crush on William before they even met.

19

CHAPTER 8

They Meet

After graduating from Eton College, William took time off to go to Chile. He worked in an area far away from everything, painting houses and scrubbing toilets. He then decided to go to the University of Saint Andrews in Scotland the next year.

Kate took a year off to go to Italy and study Italian. Afterward, she also decided to go to the University of Saint Andrews.

William and Kate lived in the same dorm building on different floors. They were both enrolled as art history majors.

At the University of Saint Andrews, William dated Kate's friend, Carly Massy-Birch, for six weeks. Kate dated a senior named Rupert Finch.

William working in Chile in 2000

It wasn't long before William invited some students to his dorm room to hang out. Kate was one of them.

After the first year, both William and Kate thought about going to different schools. Prince Charles, William's father, told him to try to stick it out for another year. Kate's parents told her the same thing. Kate and William, now friends, both took that advice. They encouraged each other to join clubs and try new activities.

William loves to ride horses and play polo, a game played on horseback. Kate is allergic to horses.

Toward the end of the year, William encouraged Kate to be in a charity fashion show. After the show, he began thinking of her differently. Soon, they were boyfriend and girlfriend.

The University of Saint Andrews, where
William and Kate went to school together.

CHAPTER 9

At Last

From 2002 to 2007, William and Kate dated. They finished their last three years at Saint Andrews together. When they graduated, William went into military training. Kate tried starting an Internet business. Then she became a fashion buyer for the store Jigsaw. What she really wanted was to marry William. But he wasn't ready yet.

William gave Kate a diamond and sapphire ring when they got engaged. The ring had belonged to his mother.

When Kate wasn't with him, William worried. She had protection from the paparazzi when they were together. But when she was alone,

William and Kate dated happily for many years.

they bothered her. William didn't want Kate to get hurt. Since he couldn't protect her, he thought it was best to break up. But that didn't last for long.

William missed Kate. She was sad but was trying to move on. Finally, William couldn't take being away from Kate. He took Kate on a vacation to Kenya, Africa, and asked her to marry him on October 19, 2010.

William married Kate on April 29, 2011. William wore his military uniform. Kate wore a simple ivory, or off-white, dress with lace. The Queen lent her a real diamond tiara to wear to hold her veil.

William and Kate were married in Westminster Abbey, where William's parents were married.

The couple kissed before a crowd of thousands outside Buckingham Palace. At last, they were husband and wife.

William and Kate ride back to Buckingham Palace after their wedding.

CHAPTER 10

Happily Ever After

William and Kate's fairy tale was off to a good start. William decided to stay in the military for now. He is a helicopter pilot and flies rescue missions.

Kate is following in Princess Diana's footsteps by making appearances and helping charities. Kate and William hope to have children one day.

William may be king in the future. But William's grandmother is the current Queen Elizabeth II. And his father, Prince Charles, is next in line to the throne. Both are in good health. So William probably won't become king for a long time.

For now, the new royal couple are living happily.

William and Kate are planning a happy future together.

GLOSSARY

boarding school (BORE-ding SKOOL): A boarding school is a school at which students receive their lodging and meals for the term. Kate and William both went to boarding school.

charities (CHAR-i-tees): Charities are organizations that provide money or assistance to those in need. Princess Diana often gave money and support to charities.

dorm (DORM): *Dorm* is short for *dormitory*, which is a building for housing students at a college. William lived in a dorm at Saint Andrews University.

heir (AIR): An heir is a person who inherits a title or throne. The heir to the throne of the United Kingdom is Prince Charles.

paparazzi (pah-puh-RAHT-see): Photographers who take pictures of celebrities for publication are members of the paparazzi. The paparazzi chased Princess Diana in her car.

tiaras (tee-AIR-uhz): Tiaras are crowns that a queen or princess wears. Kate wore one of Queen Elizabeth's tiaras made of diamonds at her wedding.

FURTHER INFORMATION

BOOKS

Bingham, Jane. *William and Kate: A Royal Romance*. Florida: Raintree, 2011.

Cooke, C. W. and Szyksznian, Michael. *The Royals: Prince William & Kate Middleton Graphic Novel Edition*. Vancouver, WA: Bluewater Productions, 2011.

Tracey, Kathleen. *Prince William.* Hockessin, DE: Mitchell Lane Publishers, 2011.

WEB SITES

Visit our Web site for links about William and Kate: childsworld.com/links

Note to Parents, Teachers, and Librarians: We routinely verify our Web links to make sure they are safe and active sites. So encourage your readers to check them out!

INDEX

ABOUT THE AUTHOR

Dale-Marie Bryan is a former elementary teacher and
the author of several books for children. She writes
from the home she shares with her husband and many
pets in southeast Kansas.